NATURE CLOSE-UP

Ant Lions

and Lacewings

TEXT BY ELAINE PASCOE

PHOTOGRAPHS BY DWIGHT KUHN

BLACKBIRCH PRESS

An imprint of Thomson Gale, a part of The Thomson Corporation

THOMSON

GALE

Detroit • New York • San Francisco • San Diego • New Haven, Conn. • Waterville, Maine • London • Munich

LIBRARY OF CONGRESS CATALOGING-IN-PUBLICATION DATA

Pascoe, Elaine.
  Ant lions and lacewings / by Elaine Pascoe ; photographs by Dwight Kuhn.
    p. cm. — (Nature close-up)
  Includes index.
  ISBN 1-4103-0310-1 (alk. paper)
  1. Ant lions and lacewings—Juvenile literature. I. Kuhn, Dwight. II. Title III. Series:
Pascoe, Elaine. Nature close-up.

Printed in China
10 9 8 7 6 5 4 3 2 1

Contents

1

Fierce Hunters

An ant scurries across a patch of sandy ground. Its path takes it to the rim of a little funnel-shaped pit. As it steps over the rim, the sand gives way under its feet, and the ant tumbles down into the pit. It tries to climb out, but an avalanche of sand knocks it back down.

The pit is a trap made by an ant lion, or doodlebug. The doodlebug is hiding in the bottom. Only its sharp, pincer-like jaws stick out of the sand. It grabs the ant in its jaws and drags its prey under the sand.

Ant lions are members of a fascinating group of insects. Lacewings, owl flies, dobsonflies, and fish flies are also members of this group. These insects are found in many parts of the world. Although they are harmless to people, in the insect world they are fierce **predators**.

An adult ant lion (right) looks very different from an ant lion larva (opposite, catching an ant).

5

An adult ant lion has wings, long antennae, and big compound eyes.

Family Traits

Ant lions and their relatives share a number of traits. Like all insects, they have six legs and three body sections—head, **thorax**, and abdomen. Instead of a bony skeleton, they have an outer skin called an **exoskeleton**. They feel and taste with antennae located on the head. And they see the world through **compound eyes**, with many lenses.

6

As adults, these insects have two pairs of delicate wings that are crisscrossed by veins. The veins look like a network of nerves, and that gave rise to the scientific name for this insect group: *Neuroptera*, or nerve wing. With their wings and long, thin bodies, the adults look like small dragonflies or damselflies. But unlike those insects, they can fold their wings back over their bodies when they are not flying.

As **larvae**, they do not have wings. But they have strong, sharp jaws, or **mandibles**. They use those jaws to catch their prey.

An ant lion larva has powerful jaws, which it uses to catch prey.

Ant Lions

Ant lions are common in the United States, especially in the South and the Southwest. They are found in other parts of the world as well. Warm, dry regions with sandy soil are perfect for these insects.

As adults, ant lions are **nocturnal**. They are not strong fliers. But they are attracted to light, so they can sometimes be seen at windows and porch lights on summer nights. An adult ant lion is about 1.5 inches (3.8 cm) long and gray or brownish gray in color. It has large antennae with clublike knobs at the tips.

Despite their big wings, adult ant lions are not very good fliers.

Young ant lions look completely different from the adults. An ant lion larva has an oval, flattened abdomen. Its thorax is short. And its flat head sports a pair of outsized, crescent-shaped jaws. The larvae are nicknamed doodlebugs, but it's not clear how they got that name. It may be for the twisting trails the insects leave in sand, which look like doodles.

As soon as they hatch, ant lion larvae begin looking for places to dig their traps. Although doodlebugs like sand, they'll dig in any type of soil made up of dry, loose particles.

An ant lion larva digs into loose sand tail first.

Ant lion pits are often seen in sandy soil under overhanging rocks or the eaves of houses. The insects seem to prefer places that are protected from rain, which would flood their pits.

The insect digs by circling backward, pushing its tail end into the dirt or sand. It has fine hairs on its body that curve forward, helping it slide into ground. As it digs deeper, it uses its head like a shovel to flick sand up and out of the pit. When the pit is finished, the doodlebug stays buried at the bottom with only its open jaws exposed.

This ant lion larva has caught a red velvet mite.

If an insect or small spider falls into the trap, the doodlebug flicks sand up onto the steep sides of the pit, creating tiny landslides that keep the prey from climbing out. The prey tumbles to the bottom of the pit, and the doodlebug grabs its victim with its sharp jaws. After the doodlebug drags its prey into the sand, it pierces the victim with its jaws and sucks out its body fluids. Then it flicks the insect's dry shell out of the pit.

An ant lion cocoon
is made of sticky silk
and sand.

Ant Lion Life Cycle

The doodlebug goes through several stages as it grows. At each stage, it must **molt**—it sheds its skin and steps out in a new, bigger skin. As it grows, it builds larger pits and catches larger prey. At first the pit may be less than an inch (2.5 cm) across, and the ant lion catches only very small insects. Even at their largest, the pits are only about 2 inches (5 cm) across and 2 inches deep.

When it is full grown, the doodlebug surrounds itself with a cocoon made of grains of sand and sticky strands of silk, produced by glands in its body. It becomes a pupa.

The cocoon is about a third of an inch (7 to 8 mm) across. It lies buried in the sand, while inside it the insect's body slowly changes. After a month or so, the insect breaks out of its cocoon and crawls to the surface. It is now a winged adult. It flies off in search of a mate.

After mating, female ant lions lay their eggs in dry, loose soil—where the larvae will be able to dig pits when they hatch. The entire life cycle, from egg to adult, often takes two years to complete.

A cocoon cut open shows that the larva inside has begun to change into an adult.

THE DOODLEBUG ORACLE

Children in many countries play a game with ant lions. They lean down over an ant-lion pit and chant a rhyme or sing a song that draws the ant lion out of its hiding place. The ant lion can't understand the rhyme, of course. But the sound creates vibrations that disturb grains of sand. The ant lion may pop out because it thinks it has caught a meal.

There are lots of superstitious beliefs about ant lions. In his novel *The Adventures of Tom Sawyer*, Mark Twain poked fun at these beliefs and other superstitions. Tom tries to use a magic charm to find some marbles he has lost. When the charm doesn't work, he suspects a witch is working against him. He decides to ask a doodlebug:

He searched around till he found a small sandy spot with a little funnel-shaped depression in it. He laid himself down and put his mouth close to this depression and called—
"Doodle-bug, doodle-bug, tell me what I want to know! Doodle-bug, doodle-bug, tell me what I want to know!"
The sand began to work, and presently a small black bug appeared for a second and then darted under again in a fright.
"He dasn't tell! So it was a witch that done it. I just knowed it."

Will an ant lion tell you what you want to know?

14

Lacewings

As you might guess, lacewings are named for their long, gauzy wings. The network of veins on the wings makes them look like lace. Lacewings come in two main types —brown and green—and there are many different species. These insects are found throughout North America, but brown lacewings are seen more often in the West than in the East.

Adult lacewings are less than an inch (2.5 cm) long, while the larvae grow up to about half that long. The adults are not strong fliers. With their wobbly, fluttery flight paths, they're often caught by birds and other predators.

The green lacewing is named for its delicate, gauzy wings.

A green lacewing larva has sharp jaws for piercing prey.

Adult green lacewings are pale green, with golden eyes. Their larvae are tan and covered with bumps called **tubercles**. Brown lacewing larvae are brown and smooth. Both types of larvae look a bit like tiny alligators. Both have sharp, crescent-shaped jaws for grabbing prey. And both are busy predators.

Unlike ant lions, lacewings don't build traps. Instead, they roam plants in search of prey. They prefer soft-bodied insects such as aphids and mealy bugs, but they will eat almost anything they can catch and kill. Like ant lions, lacewings pierce their prey with their sharp jaws and suck out the body fluids. They also devour insect eggs.

Usually the lacewings just leave the skins of their victims behind. But some species of brown lacewing larvae cover themselves with the skins of their victims, bits of plant matter, and other debris. This strange habit has won them the nickname "trash bug." The "trash" helps the insects. It provides **camouflage**, helping the lacewings hide from larger predators that might want to eat them.

This green lacewing
larva has caught an
aphid in its jaws.

17

Lacewing Life Cycle

Lacewings usually lay their eggs on plants. Green lacewing eggs are easy to recognize because each egg sits at the end of a thin stalk. When the eggs begin to hatch, the stalks keep the new larvae from eating one another or nearby unhatched eggs. Brown lacewing eggs don't have stalks. But they're often laid singly, so the larvae don't get a chance to attack each other.

The larvae are always hungry. They feed and grow for two or three weeks, molting several times. Then each larva finds a sheltered place under plant leaves or in leaf litter. It spins a ball-shaped silk cocoon and pupates, changing into an adult. Lacewings that pupate in fall stay in their cocoons through the winter. They come out in the spring, ready to mate and lay eggs.

Opposite: A female green lacewing lays eggs that have thin stalks.

Below: Lacewing larvae are always hunting for food.

GARDEN HELPERS

Many kinds of insects damage crops and garden plants. But many other insects help gardeners by attacking those pests. Lacewings are one of those helpers. Other garden helpers include:

A lacewing closes in on an aphid, a major garden pest.

Ground beetles — These large dark beetles feed on slugs and many kinds of insects.

Ladybugs — These spotted beetles are great predators. As larvae and adults, they prey on aphids, mealy bugs, and other small insects.

Spiders — There are many kinds of spiders, only some of which spin webs. All are hunters, and they catch many garden pests.

Wasps — Some tiny wasps are parasites. They lay their eggs in the bodies of various caterpillars and other insects. When the eggs hatch, the larvae feed on their hosts and kill them.

Some of these insects turn up in gardens naturally. But gardeners also buy beneficial insects such as lacewings, ladybugs, and parasitic wasps, and release them in their gardens. In this way they avoid using chemical pesticides that can harm the environment.

Owl Flies

Several other insects are close relatives of ant lions and lacewings. Adult *owl flies* are named for their huge, owl-like eyes. These insects are grayish brown and less than 2 inches (5 cm) long, with long knobbed antennae. Good fliers and fierce predators, they are active at night. During the day the owl fly rests on branch, looking just like a twig. When threatened, it lifts its abdomen in the air and releases a musky odor that might deter predators.

Female owl flies lay their eggs on twigs. The larvae hatch and drop to the ground. They are a lot like ant lions, but they don't dig pits. Instead, they rely on camouflage. The brownish gray larva hides in leaf litter, blending in perfectly, with its jaws wide open. When a small insect comes by, the owlfly larva grabs it.

The owl fly is named for its big owlish eyes.

A female adult dobsonfly lives just long enough to mate and lay eggs.

Dobsonflies and Fish Flies

Adult dobsonflies are fierce-looking insects, about 2 inches (5 cm) long. The males have huge jaws that almost look like tusks. It's unlikely that you'll ever see one of them. The adults are nocturnal, and they live for only a few days in summer—just long enough to mate and lay eggs. During that time, they usually do not eat. The female may bite if she is disturbed, but the male mainly uses his huge jaws to fight off other males and hold the female when they mate.

After mating, the female lays a mass of eggs on a branch overhanging a stream. She deposits a white substance on the eggs. This makes the eggs look like bird droppings, so predators don't bother them. When they hatch, the larvae drop into the stream.

The dobsonfly larva is a wormlike creature sometimes called a hellgrammite. It is aquatic—it lives completely in the water. It breathes through feathery **gills** located along its abdomen. The larva preys on various **aquatic** insects and other little water creatures. It lives two or three years in the water, growing up to 3 inches (7.5 cm) long. Then it crawls onto land and spins a cocoon. It spends the winter as a pupa. In spring, it breaks out of its cocoon for its short adult life.

The dobsonfly larva lives in water. It has strong jaws for catching prey.

The fish fly is similar to the dobsonfly but smaller and redder in color. Fishermen use the larvae of both these insects for bait. The larvae are usually found under rocks and logs in clean, fast-running streams. But they must be handled carefully because they can bite hard enough to draw blood.

An adult fish fly rests on a leaf. The larvae of this insect are sometimes used as bait.

Ant Lions, Lacewings, and People

Ant lions and their clever sand traps have fascinated people since ancient times. There are lots of old stories and rhymes about these insects. Monsters based on ant lions have even figured in some modern science fiction films. For example, in *Star Wars Episode VI: The Return of the Jedi*, the heroes are nearly devoured by a huge monster that lives at the bottom of a deep sand hole—exactly like a giant ant-lion pit.

Ant lion larvae have inspired lots of monster stories. But the real thing is much too small to hurt people.

Of course, that's fiction. In fact, ant lions and their tiny traps are harmless to people. Except for dobsonfly and fish fly larvae, which may bite if bothered, the other insects in this family are also harmless. They cause no damage to gardens or buildings. They are **beneficial** because they feed on insects that can be harmful. Lacewings are especially helpful to gardeners because they roam plants looking for aphids and other pests.

25

2

Collecting and Caring for Ant Lions and Lacewings

Ant lions and lacewings are not hard to find. Ant lions are common in warmer climates, and lacewings can be found in fields and gardens in spring and summer. The adults are often drawn to lights at night.

Spring and summer are good times to watch these insects in the wild. You can also keep ant-lion or lacewing larvae for a while, so you can study them close up. Ant-lion larvae are especially easy to keep and fascinating to watch.

Ant lions and lacewings can also be ordered through the mail from sources like those listed at the end of this book. This chapter will tell you how to collect the insects and care for them. When you have finished studying your insects, take them back to the place where you found them and release them.

Ant lions are easy to keep
and fascinating to watch.

27

Lion Hunt

Find ant lion larvae in summer by looking for their traps. Check sandy areas in backyards, playgrounds, and under the eaves of houses, looking for funnel-shaped pits. When you find a pit, you may see the insect's jaws sticking out of the sand at the bottom. The ant lion is hiding just under the surface, waiting for prey.

Catching an ant lion is easy. Just use a spoon to scoop the larva out of its home. Although the ant lion's big jaws make it look dangerous, it does not bite. You can safely hold it in your hands.

Use a spoon to pick up an ant lion larva.

Put the ant lion in a small container to take it home. To make a permanent home, fill an open container with clean, dry sand to a depth of several inches. Put the larva in its new home, and it will quickly bury itself in the sand.

Keeping an ant lion for a short time will let you study the larva up close.

Ant Lion Care

Before long, the ant lion will start to dig a pit in its new home. If you should bump the container and cause the pit to fill with sand, the insect will quickly rebuild its trap.

After the ant lion makes its pit, you should feed it an ant or some other small nonflying insect twice a week. You can find ants by looking under logs or on walkways and driveways. Scoop an ant into a small container to take it home. You can use tweezers to drop the ant directly into the ant-lion pit. Or you can just put the insect in the container and cover the top with cheesecloth and a rubber band until it is caught. Soon the ant will stumble into the pit and slide down to the ant lion's waiting jaws.

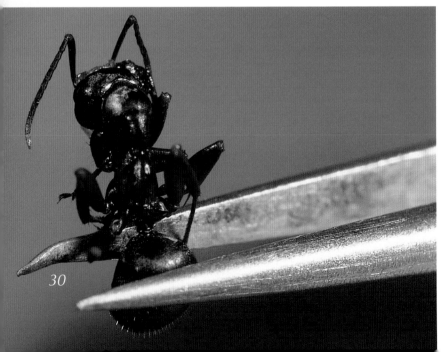

Top: Your ant lion will dig a pit in a container of sand.

Bottom: Use tweezers to feed an ant to the larva.

30

Eventually the larva will stop eating prey. The pit will start to fill in and may disappear. The larva has changed into a pupa, in a round cocoon near the bottom of the pit. In a month or so, the adult may emerge. You can cover the top of the container with cheesecloth, to keep the adult from flying off when it comes out of the sand. Check every day because the adult will not live long. You can let the adult go after you study it.

With luck, you'll see a winged adult emerge from its cocoon.

31

Looking for Lacewings

To find lacewing larvae, look on garden plants and in fields where weeds and bushes grow. The larvae patrol plants for aphids, so look for them on plants where aphids are found. Aphids cluster on many garden plants, often on the undersides of leaves. Most are green, but they may be black, gray, brown, pink, yellow, or other colors.

Clip stems and leaves with aphids and lacewing larvae on them, and put them in a small container to take home. The lacewings will need the aphids for food, and the aphids will need the juices in the plant stems and leaves.

You can also collect lacewing eggs, or you can buy the eggs from mail-order sources. To collect eggs, look on the undersides of leaves of plants where you see aphids. Green lacewing eggs are easy to identify. They are carried on little stalks about 1/4 inch (0.6 cm) long. Clip a leaf with eggs and a section of the plant with aphids on it. The eggs will hatch in just a few days, and the new larvae will need food right away.

Check plants where aphids are found to locate lacewing larvae and eggs.

Inset: A green lacewing egg attached to the underside of a leaf.

Lacewing Care

At home, set up a container for your lacewings. Put the stem with aphids in the container, and then add the eggs or larvae you have collected. New lacewing larvae are tiny. To keep them from escaping, put a cover on the container. Punch tiny holes in the container to let air in. You can use a small nail to make the holes. For larger larvae, cover the container with mesh, secured by a rubber band.

Lacewing larvae need a steady of supply of aphids to feed on. Every few days you will have to collect fresh stems with aphids for your lacewings. Remove all the old stems, gently brushing the larvae back into the container. Then add the new stems and aphids.

A lacewing larva will grow about half an inch (12 to 13 mm) long. Eventually it forms a white cocoon. Place the cocoon in a clean, dry container, and put some small twigs in with it. One day an adult lacewing will hatch out of the cocoon. The adult will climb up a twig and spread its wings to dry. Cover your container with mesh and a rubber band, so you can see the adult before it flies off. But when the wings dry, let the lacewing fly away to finish its life cycle in the wild.

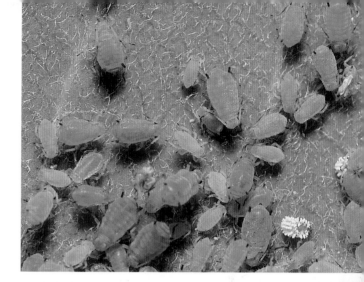

Top: To feed lacewing larvae, you'll need lots of aphids.

Bottom: Put a lacewing cocoon in a clean container with twigs and a mesh cover.

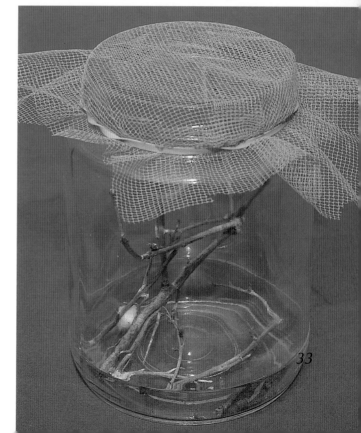

33

3

Investigating Doodlebugs
and Lacewings

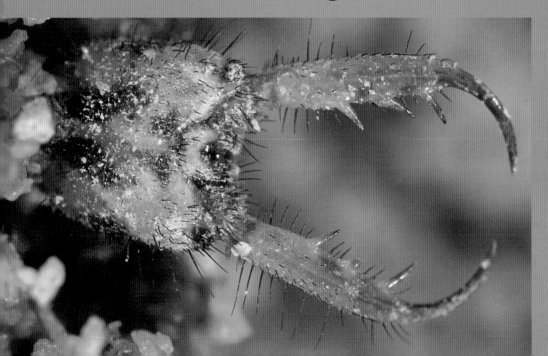

In this section, you'll find some projects and activities that will help you learn more about ant lions and lacewings. Some of these activities can be done with doodlebugs, and some with lacewing larvae. Have fun with these activities. When you're finished, remember to return any insects you've collected to the places where you found them.

What Materials Do Doodlebugs Like for Their Pits?

To most people, dirt is dirt. But to a doodlebug, having the right kind of soil makes all the difference when it comes to making a successful trap. Based on what you know about these animals, decide what materials you think they prefer. Then do this activity to see if you are right.

What to Do:

1. Put equal amounts of the different materials in the container. Try to keep the materials separate.
2. Using a spoon, place your ant lion larva in the center.

35

Results: Watch to see where the larva eventually digs its pit. What material did it prefer?

Conclusion: Why do you think the ant lion chooses one material over the others? Repeat the experiment with other ant lions, to see if you get different results. You can also try this experiment using different materials, such as sugar and ground coffee. Or try it with wet sand and dry sand. Separate the wet and dry sand with a piece of wood or plastic, and see which the doodlebug prefers.

36

Do Doodlebugs Prefer Open Spaces or Sheltered Places?

When doodlebugs go scouting for home sites, location is important. What suits a doodlebug best—a site that's open to the sky or under some type of shelter? Make your best guess, based on what you've read about these insects. Then test your answer by doing this activity.

What to Do:

1. Put an even layer of sand, several inches deep, in the container.
2. Cover half of the container with a towel or piece of cardboard. Leave the other half open.
3. Place an ant lion larva in the center, and see where it goes.

Results: Watch to see where the larva builds its home. Repeat the experiment with several different doodlebugs. How many choose the open side of the container? How many choose the covered side?

Conclusion: Based on your results, what sort of sites do you think doodlebugs prefer? Where would you be most likely to find them in the wild?

What You Need:
- Wide, shallow container
- Sand
- Ant lion larva

How Many Aphids Does a Lacewing Larva Eat in 24 Hours?

Lacewing larvae are known for their big appetites. How many aphids do you think one of these predators can put away over a 24-hour period? Decide what you think, and then do this activity to find out.

What to Do:

1. Put the stem with aphids in the container. Count the aphids on the stem, and make a note of the number.
2. Add a large lacewing larva to the container.
3. Cover the jar with cheesecloth and a rubber band.
4. Check the container in 24 hours, and count how many aphids are still alive.

Results: How many aphids did the lacewing eat?

Conclusion: Based on your results, how effective do you think lacewing larvae would be in controlling aphids in the garden? Try repeating this experiment several times, and see if you get the same results. If your results vary, can you think of reasons why?

Will Lacewing Larvae That Have More Food Form Cocoons Sooner than Those Fed Less?

Lacewing larvae feed and grow for two or three weeks before making cocoons and pupating. Does a larva's food supply affect the time of this change? Make your best guess, and then do this experiment to test your answer.

What You Need:
- Two clean containers
- Cheesecloth and rubber bands, to cover the containers
- Two lacewing larvae, both the same size
- Plant stem with six aphids on it
- Second plant stem with 20 or more aphids

What to Do:

1. Put the stem with six aphids in one container. Put the stem with 20 or more aphids in the second container.
2. Add a lacewing larva to each container. Be sure the larvae are the same size.
3. Cover the containers with cheesecloth and rubber bands. Keep them side by side, so the temperature and other conditions will be the same for both.

39

4. Every day, replace the old stems with new ones carrying fresh aphids. Each time, put only a few aphids in the first container and many aphids in the second.

5. Check every day to see how the larvae develop and when they build their cocoons. Keep a journal and note the changes you see.

Results: Note which larva builds its cocoon first.

Conclusion: What do your results tell you about the role that food supply plays in the lacewing's life cycle?

More Activities with Ant Lions and Lacewings

1. Remove a doodlebug from its home in the sand and place it on a new sandy area. Use a hand lens to examine the insect's body and see how it moves. How does it burrow into the sand? Check back often over the next few hours watching how it builds its new pit.

2. Place your doodlebugs on other substances besides sand. Try using sugar instead, for example. The white color allows you to see the insect clearly. What does the doodlebug do?

3. Find out how far doodlebugs fling the sand when they make their pits. Put some dark paper on a table. Place one doodlebug in a shallow cup filled with sand, and put the cup in the center of the paper. Give the insect a day to make a pit, and then measure how far the sand is flung from the pit.

4. Look for lacewing eggs on plants in the garden or a field. You'll have the best luck on plants that have aphids. Where are the eggs mostly found—on the tops or undersides of leaves, or on the stems? Count the number of eggs you find at different locations on the plant. Use a hand lens to watch eggs to see if larvae hatch. This usually happens in late morning. The eggs turn from green to white and often show some striping as they get close to hatching.

5. Look for lacewing larvae on plants. Again, you'll generally find them on plants with aphids. Use a hand lens to watch the insects as they hunt for prey. Can you tell if they are green lacewings or brown lacewings? How does the larva eat? How long does it take to finish its meal?

Results and Conclusions

Here are some possible results and conclusions for the activities on pages 34 to 42. Many factors may affect the results of these activities. If your results differ, try to think of reasons why. Repeat the activity with different conditions, and see if your results change.

What materials do doodlebugs like for their pits?
Ant-lion larvae usually prefer fine-textured, dry materials, like fine dry sand or sugar. Texture and size are more important than what the material is. Fine dry materials crumble easily when prey steps into the ant lion's pit.

Do doodlebugs prefer open spaces or sheltered places?
In the wild, doodlebugs usually choose sites that are sheltered rather than in the open. The shelter helps protect their pits from being destroyed by rain. But some doodlebugs don't seem to have strong preferences about this, so your results may vary.

How many aphids does a lacewing larva eat in 24 hours?
Results will vary. A lacewing may eat 100 to 600 aphids during its two- to three-week larval stage. But the number eaten on any given day depends on many factors, including the size of the larva (a large larva eats more) and the size of the aphids. Even the temperature will affect your results. Like other insects, lacewing larvae are more active and thus eat more in warm temperatures.

Will lacewing larvae that have more food form cocoons sooner than those fed less?
Lacewings that have all the food they can eat are likely to grow faster and pupate sooner than those that have less food.

Some Words About Doodlebugs and Lacewings

aquatic Living in water.

beneficial Helpful.

camouflage Coloring and patterns that help living things blend in with their surroundings.

compound eyes Eyes that have many lenses, or facets.

environment The surroundings and conditions that affect living things and their ability to survive.

exoskeleton The hard outer skin of an insect. It takes the place of an internal skeleton.

gills Organs that allow an animal to get oxygen from water.

larvae Young or immature insects.

mandibles Jaws.

molt To shed the skin.

nocturnal Active at night.

predators Animals that kill and eat other animals.

thorax The center section of an insect's body. Usually the legs and wings are attached here.

tubercles Knoblike bumps.

Sources for Doodlebugs and Lacewings

You can buy ant-lion and lacewing larvae, and lacewing eggs, through the mail. Here are some sources:

Doodlebugs

AntLionFarms.com
4509 Chantilly Way
Pensacola, FL 32505
(877) 332-8706
www.antlionfarms.com

Lacewings

Gardens Alive!
5100 Schenley Place
Lawrenceburg, IN 47025
(812) 537-8650
www.gardensalive.com

Planet Natural
1612 Gold Ave.
Bozeman, MT 59715
(800) 289-6656
www.planetnatural.com/
beneficialinsects1.html

Rincon-Vitova Insectaries, Inc.
PO Box 1555
Ventura, CA 93002
(800) 243-2847
www.rinconvitova.com

For More Information

Books

Discovery Channel Science, *Insects*. Milwaukee, WI: Gareth Stevens, 2002.

Sally Kneidel, *Creepy Crawlies and the Scientific Method: More than 100 Hands-On Science Experiments for Children*. Golden, CO: Fulcrum, 1993.

Allison Mia Starcher, *Good Bugs for Your Garden*. Chapel Hill, NC: Algonquin Books, 1995.

Sara Van Dyck, *Insect Wars*. Danbury, CT: Franklin Watts, 1997.

Christina Wilsdon, *Insects* (National Audubon Society First Field Guide). New York, NY: Scholastic, Inc., 1995

Websites

Alien Empire
www.pbs.org/wnet/nature/alienempire
Explore the world of insects at this Public Broadcasting System site.

The Antlion Pit
www.antlionpit.com
Learn about ant lions and see videos of doodlebugs feeding at this site.

Index